AWAKE, ARISE,

OR BE FOREVER FALLEN!

Alberto Vezendi

Awake, Arise,
or be forever fallen!

Vezendi  BOOKS

My dear children,
you're not old enough yet to listen to my
story and I can't know for sure that I'll still be
around by the time you grow up, so I've put
it down here for you — lest it should go away
with me for good. I'm the only one who can
do this because I'm the only one who knows
— well, almost, for She does too —
but She would never tell.
And She's the silent kind, anyway.

INTRODUCTION

He who should teach men to die
would at the same time teach them to live.
MICHEL DE MONTAIGNE, *Essays*[2]

This book is about my personal experience as a young anorexic male, but it carries a message of hope for all: that a better life is possible, regardless of your situation, and that you already have everything you need to live it. It's all inside your mind.

I went from having a carefree joy-filled life to falling into the depths of intellectual and physical misery, where death became my only companion, and then rose from my own ashes to become a better person than I ever was before.

For twenty years, I rode on a fairly tolerable rollercoaster of elation and melancholy. But one day something went wrong. I flew off my seat and began to plummet into the darkest abyss of my mind on a freefall of anorexic self-destruction. The disorder dragged me into the depths of abject misery, until I hit rock bottom. That was the turning point: I had to choose between construction and destruction, between living and dying.

I chose to live.

Imminent death brought me back to life and also lifted the veil from my eyes, exposing to me my real self. I had to accept that the pathetic anorexic living corpse I saw before me was no one but myself. Not the false attractive image of myself I had been imagining through the lens of more than twenty years of unremitting conditioning, combined with the much deeper distortion caused by anorexia, but my real self at last.

Accepting myself as I really am meant the beginning of a new life — the first step in the long journey to rescue the wreck that I had become, rehabilitate it into a man, and rise to a new existence of conscious bliss.

Change can come from inspiration or from desperation. I had to go through the tortuous road of desperation before I woke up and saw the light. It was a painful road that I wish no one should ever have to endure.

Just as we don't need to burn our own hands to know that we shouldn't place them on a hot stove, because others have done so before and shared their experience with us so that we don't have to learn this the hard way, I decided to show my blisters to the world in this book, in the hope that this will help readers avoid falling into a trap created by their own mind.

And that is precisely the reason which led me to write this book: to inspire you, dear reader, to find the light inside of you, without having to cut through your inner darkness with the rough chisel of deep trauma, or to endure a long and painful rite of passage like the one I went through.

That light within is called life, and it's the only light that can guide you to happiness. But it's a light that can only shine in the present, and this book is a challenge to live fully that present moment called life.

There's no better time than now to break the spell that binds us to a life of zombie-like aimless roaming, like animated corpses; no better time to tear to pieces the bandage that blindfolds our eyes, preventing us from seeing the paradise we're living in; no better time to start living the life we were meant to live: a life of freedom, of bliss, of self-actualization.

The magic is in you: just open your heart and you'll see it.

Welcome to paradise!

PART · I

THE DEVIL WITHIN,
OR HOW MY MIND TRIED TO KILL ME

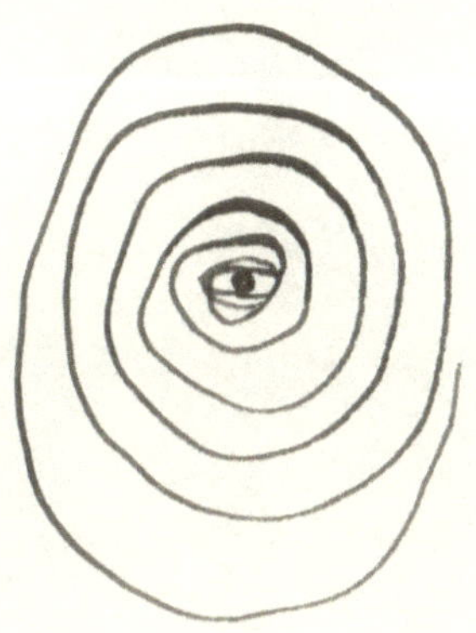

A man's mind may make him a Buddha,
or it may make him a beast.
Therefore, control your mind
and do not let it deviate from the right path.

From The Teaching of Buddha[3]

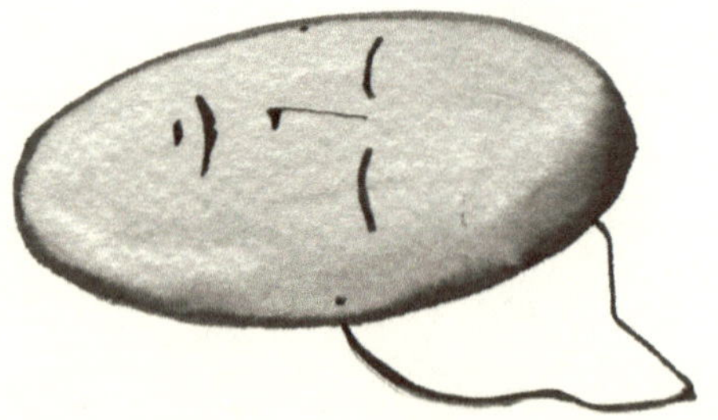

THE GESTATION

Be who you are and say what you feel,
because those who mind don't matter,
and those who matter don't mind.

BERNARD BARUCH[*]

At some point in my teens, a thick pall of obsessions began to gradually cover all the light in my life until after a few years all that was left was darkness.

For no obvious reason, I started to skid down a steep slope — slowly, almost imperceptibly at first — but quickly gathering momentum, until it was too late to stop. After sliding totally out of control, I was sucked into the quicksand of self-deception from which only a shock could blast me out.

That shock eventually came, otherwise I would not be writing these lines.

It all started in the summer of 1995, when I was 22 years old, in what is supposed to be the prime of one's life. I had just returned from an Erasmus year at a university in Northern Ireland and was looking forward to a fun-filled summer by the ocean in my hometown in the northwest of Spain.

I had everything a man could wish for in order to be happy: health, friends, girlfriends, money, time, freedom. I was doing well in my studies. Life was easy. And yet it was precisely at this time that my disorder set in.

The disorder did not, however, come out of the blue: I had seen it coming for a long, long time.

In my childhood, I had the rare ability to find happiness everywhere I was, for the simple reason — as I realized much later — that I instinctively drew all my happiness from within. I had friends, I was outgoing, I found it easy to communicate with the people around me, and I was always helpful and supportive. But I didn't need anybody, and I didn't really want anything from anyone.

Being so young, I didn't understand then where the magic came from, but now I do. We can only be happy if we are ourselves. And being yourself requires the amoral honesty and strength to be unconcerned with other people's opinions about how you're leading your life.

Nightcrawler

> *We are strange beings, we seem to go free,
> but we go in chains — chains of training,
> custom, convention, association, environment
> — in a word, circumstance, and against these
> bonds the strongest of us struggle in vain.*
> MARK TWAIN[5]

Then something odd began to happen. Somewhere in my late teens, I began to change, I started to want to fit in, and, inch by inch, I started giving in to other people's wishes.

As I was later to find out, the underlying reason for that change was deeply embedded in the most remote layers of my mind, in the form of conditioning and fixed ideas.

So far in my life, I had been immune to almost every external influence: I listened attentively to what people were saying and fully respected their opinions, but I somehow managed to filter those stimuli, discard them or learn from them, and still remain myself.

At least that's what I thought. But life proved me wrong. What I did not realize was that all those external inducements had sneaked through the filters I was applying and had installed themselves in my subconscious mind.

The friction stemming from the dissonance between the external expectations about what my life should have been, and what it really was, had been building up silently but inexorably for many years. And yet, the process went mostly unnoticed because all along the line I somehow managed to suppress that inner conflict. I fooled myself into thinking that I was in control, what I didn't know was that none of those repressed thoughts vanished: they all remained firmly rooted in my subconscious mind and soon started to ramify, to gain momentum, with the pressure increasing by the day.

And just like the pressure of a river confined by a dam silently grows until one day it finds a weakness in the concrete structure and breaks through, all the repressed dormant conditioning suddenly burst its way into my conscious mind.

For the first time in my life, I began to look for happiness outside. I sought external validation, I wanted to please others, I wanted to be liked. And I was liked, too, but at the expense of my own freedom, for I stopped being myself.

The resulting repression of my own self developed into a habit. I got used to living in this permanent state of self-denial. I had, in fact, lost my real self. For everything I turned myself into belonged to someone else — it was their appreciation, their expectations, their idea of my happiness, their love, their time.

During those years, from the outside, everything still seemed to be just perfect, but on the inside, I knew that things were not going right. Something was happening: I could feel it but was unable to identify it. Despite having every reason to be happy, I felt no happiness within.

Something essential was now missing from my life: meaning. Before the change, I had a clear objective in life: to be a writer. Writing filled my lonesome hours with joy and that was enough to give my life a purpose and a sense of direction. But to be able to write I had to be myself, and I wasn't anymore. Deep down, I knew that my life was meant to be different, I knew that I was living somebody else's life, I knew I was rolling along on the easy path of imitation, doing just what everybody else around me was doing. My family and my friends seemed happy enough with that, but I was not.

I began to want more and more, but I did not even know what it was I wanted. I was no longer at the helm of my own life. I had started to drift until I totally lost direction. There was a widening gap between what I really was and the idolized image of myself I aimed at becoming. My whole personal existence had slowly dissolved into a meaningless void.

The emptiness that had been slowly growing inside had now surfaced and invaded my entire being. I tried to fill it with all kinds of distractions, including drugs, but the harder I tried to close the gap, the larger it became, until it eventually grew into a gaping chasm that sucked me into it.

I imagine Carlos Castaneda's Don Juan's halos of mystical light as perfect spheres around every living creature. Mine was shattered, and the darkness seeping through the cracks began to extinguish my light. I felt lost and empty. The

disease had stealthily crept into my world — like
a nightcrawler.

THE DISEASE

In the beginning of the malady it is easy to cure but difficult to detect, but in the course of time, not having been either detected or treated in the beginning, it becomes easy to detect but difficult to cure.

NICCOLÒ MACHIAVELLI, *The Prince*[6]

In Middle English, the word "disease" meant "lack of ease; inconvenience", from the Old French word *desaise*, a synonym for "malaise", which, according to the Oxford English Dictionary, means: "a general feeling of discomfort, illness, or unease whose exact cause is difficult to identify".

And that's exactly what I was going through. Although I had every reason to be happy, and despite all the external signs of happiness, I felt a permanent malaise. I lost sight of the magical beauty of existence, and started to feel persistent mental and physical discomfort. And since by that time I had already lost all perspective on who I really was,

I surrendered to that malaise. It became a constant feature of my life, to the point that I completely forgot the state of blissful happiness I had once been living in.

Since I'd lost my own inner goal in life, I had to seek validation outside, in the approval of the people around me. I began to compare myself with others, with the result that I stopped wanting to be just good, and started to want to be better — and wanting to be better inevitably led to wanting to be perfect. I soon fell into the trap of obsessive behaviors. I became addicted to people telling me how good I was at this and at that, how skillfully I performed a certain task. Their appreciation seemed to be the only thing that could fill that emptiness, so I quickly developed an obsession for work and excellence in the hope of reaping recognition.

I soon became a relentless perfectionist, and like all perfectionists, I, too, lived my days in a perpetual state of frustration. Not only had I to keep myself busy all the time so that I could not think, but I also had to do everything immediately, and the result had to be just perfect.

As well as that, I began to feel guilty every time I had to rest or sleep. So I reduced inactive periods to the strict minimum, and, of course, banned all leisure and relaxation activities.

The obsession grew so powerful that it deceived me into thinking that I finally had a purpose in life. It kept me so busy that almost unwittingly I forgot all my problems: I simply had no time to reflect upon them. But they were still there, hidden beneath the surface, and growing.

Meanwhile, the mental and physical exertion, together with the lack of sleep and fun, was fast leading me to a state of burnout. My obsession with perfectionism had quickly filled my days, but with the same speed had also depleted my mind and my body.

Soon, I had completely lost touch with reality. I had become a robot obeying the commands of a purposeless self-imposed slavery. I had totally ceased to enjoy life; indeed, I had become so engulfed by my own obsession that I came to believe that any meaning of my existence was commensurate with the extent of my suffering. Masochistic self-denial — devoid of any trace of altruism — had become my only pleasure in life. As time went by, that obsession would develop into anorexia.

In the beginning, eating or not eating had no psychological implications. Losing weight was just the natural physical side-effect of my hyperactivity, of the imbalance between the energy input and the output, for I was using up far more calories than I was getting from my food.

As I began to associate fasting with work and eating with leisure, devoting time to eating soon became just another luxury that I couldn't afford. I simply felt guilty for not applying that time to work.

The greatest irony was that I had actually no real work to do. I was getting excellent grades in my studies with so little effort that I had to impose upon myself artificially created and totally useless tasks to fill my days, and so, find relief in idiotic mortification of the self.

I imagine that is what workaholics do. But in my case there was more to it: I was never satisfied — regardless of the actual amount of work I would do. I always had the feeling that I wasn't working enough, that I wasn't sacrificing myself enough, that I wasn't torturing myself enough.

Gradually, losing weight ceased to be merely a collateral effect of restless obsessive work and became the objective. Finally, I'd found a sense of purpose: I had a goal to fight for, albeit a pathetic one, and — like with everything else — I was doing my utmost to achieve perfection.

I began to grow fond of my new emaciated look, which gave me a permanent air of suffering. It all made sense to my sick mind: to attain perfection, the gruesome performance of my self-destruction had to be staged in the macabre circus that was my life. I had reached the point in which it was not enough to be a martyr, but I also had to look like one.

By then, I had disappeared from the world and the disorder had usurped my place.

THE FALL
—ANOREXIA NERVOSA

*The demon of worldly desires is always seeking
chances to deceive the mind. If a viper lives in your
room and you wish to have a peaceful sleep,
you must first chase it out.*
From The Teaching of Buddha[3]

"Anorexia nervosa", or simply "anorexia" — a term from the Greek, meaning "without appetite" — is classified as a mental disorder characterized mainly by behavioral patterns, such as the strict reduction of food intake; an insurmountable fear of putting on weight (regardless of one's real energy needs or appearance); an excessive preoccupation with one's body, combined with the inability to perceive objectively one's true physical appearance (i.e. a totally distorted vision of oneself); and a total lack of recognition of the disorder.

The seriousness of anorexia stems from the fact that it engulfs your entire life. You don't *suffer* from anorexia: it's so deeply entrenched in your mind that you become one with the disease. You can't just live normally while obeying the dictates of your anorexic mind: every day, from dawn till dusk, all your thoughts converge on one obsession: to lose weight. All the rest becomes secondary.

I believe it is useful to give an insight into the world of anorexia from my personal experience, as a male. I have found few testimonials by men with anorexia nervosa, which is, in a way, understandable, since this condition affects mostly women — indeed, according to statistics, more than 90% of the diagnosed cases of anorexia are female. However, statistics aside, I believe that the proportion of anorexic males is way above that meager 10% of cases, and that the reason for that number is that fewer males are actually diagnosed with anorexia.

The severity of anorexia is often overlooked, even though anorexia has the highest fatality rate of any psychological disorder — the mortality rate being 11 to 12 times greater than in the general population, and the suicide risk 56 times higher. Furthermore, only half of all recorded patients with anorexia make a full recovery.

In the United States alone, the estimated number of people who suffer from an eating disorder is 30 million. But gloomy as this statistical picture may appear, in real terms, the situation is probably much worse, mainly for two reasons.

First, because statistics only account for reported and treated cases. And second, because people suffering from anorexia, especially males, are often stigmatized, which leads to underreporting of the condition.

As with every psychological disorder, each case is different, and each person requires individual diagnosis and treatment. So what you will read here may or may not apply to others, but it is the story of my personal experience of this disorder.

The origin of my anorexia was 100% psychological. Hard as I tried, I could find nothing in the real physical world around me at that time which could have directly caused my anorexia. As I said before, my external circumstances were ideal by all standards, but what I failed to mention was that there was no bodily motive either. I always had what people tend to consider a nice physique — a lean, well-built, athletic body, with strong bones and a sinewy aspect.

The whole disorder started and developed exclusively in my mind, and all the suffering I endured was caused by my mind. Since the disorder came from my mind, the solution could only come

from the same place too. And it was indeed in my
mind that I would eventually find the way out of
the darkness and into a new life.

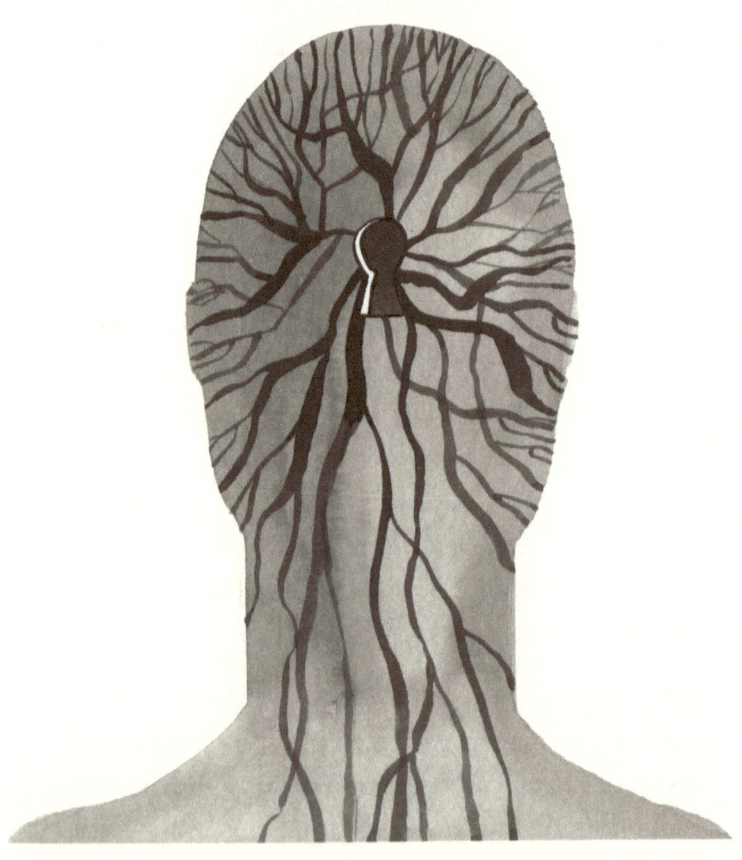

The Rituals

Nothing is so contagious as the plague; and, fanaticism, no matter of what nature, what is it but a plague of the mind?

GIACOMO CASANOVA, *Memoirs*[7]

After the initial phase of natural weight loss as a result of overwork, which lasted about 10 or 12 months, some early signs of the disorder started to manifest. First, these were diffuse and sporadic anorexic reactions that went mostly unnoticed, even by me. Soon, these reactions gave place to more frequent, conscious and even premeditated anorexia-imposed behaviors. Their frequency and intensity rose exponentially, invading and determining my life. In the worst years, my whole existence was dominated by anorexia-related thoughts and actions.

Finally, my days were becoming a never-ending

succession of compulsive rituals that I performed with fanatical devotion and ruthless perfection in a vicious ceremony of physical self-immolation on the altar of my almighty anorexic mind.

I stopped eating when I was hungry and started to eat exclusively according to a strict schedule of meals. Before developing anorexia, I would eat five or six times a day, or whenever I felt hungry. But soon I reduced this to three meals a day, then two, and in the worst years there were days when I ate only once — my meals typically consisting of tiny portions of unwholesome food.

If I felt hungry between meals, I'd drink compulsively until I'd filled my stomach with water. I would often drink all day long, convinced that it had the triple effect of quenching my thirst, cutting my appetite and cleansing my body. This manic binge drinking of water was the first symptom to appear, and the last to disappear.

Drinking a lot of water is supposed to be healthy, but the compulsive way most anorexics do it is not. In the worst years of the anorexia, I was drinking between 8 and 10 liters of water per day (between 17 and 21 US pints), often more.

I carried a full 1.5-liter bottle at all times (about 3.17 US pints), felt a desperate craving for water whenever it was half empty, and outright panic when I emptied it. I became so addicted to drowning my hunger in water that the mere prospect of not being able to drink enough made me renounce all activities in which water would not be readily available.

Sometimes, when I knew I would be eating with family or friends, I would drink the entire 1.5-liter bottle in the quarter of an hour before the meal. Naturally, by the time the meal started, there was not much room left in my stomach for any food.

Apart from fasting and drinking compulsively, day by day I increased my physical activity so I could burn more and more calories, many more than I was furnishing my body with. And with time this became more acute. If I was to draw a line graph of the chronological evolution of my physical activity and my food intake, while the former rose exponentially to the sky, the latter plummeted into a deep shaft.

I have purposely used the expression "physical activity", and not "sports", because what I was doing had nothing to do with sports. I would do anything, no matter how crazy, as far as it allowed me to burn more calories. So much so that the means soon became unimportant; only the result mattered.

For instance, I'd take three or four cold showers a day. I'd bathe in the cold ocean in the winter. I stopped using elevators. I always stood, never sat. I studied for my exams while walking. From having been an avid reader in the past, I would now only read books in situations where I had no choice but to be still, such as when travelling on buses or planes.

When eating in company, I would often excuse myself in the middle of a meal, go out to the street, and run a couple of laps around the block. And, of course, I couldn't be still or rest after eating anything, no matter how light, so after each and every meal, I *had* to walk, run or swim — compulsively.

I'd wake up early and go to sleep late, even if I had nothing to do. I always dressed too lightly for the weather in order to feel cold and in this way force my body to keep warm by burning more calories. I also started using laxatives and diuretics.

Living with anorexia was no fun...no fun at all.

For people who've never suffered an eating disorder, all these actions might seem preposterous, but sadly they are but the tip of the iceberg of the virtually unlimited range of behaviors induced by the self-destructive psychiatric condition known as anorexia nervosa.

In a very informative piece of research about the Management of Really Sick Patients with Anorexia Nervosa (MARSIPAN), conducted in 2014 by the *Royal Colleges of Psychiatrists, Physicians and Pathologists of the United Kingdom*, several cases are reported as examples of pathological anorexic behaviors that can be fatal if not properly managed by medical and psychiatric staff. The following are quotes from this research:

> "Patients with anorexia nervosa can seem deceptively well. They may have an extremely powerful drive to exercise, which sometimes seems to override their lack of nutritional reserve, so that they may appear very energetic right up to a physical collapse. One patient was seen going around a medical ward, cheerily waving to other patients through their windows, just a few days before collapsing from fatal hypoglycemia."

> "…patients with eating disorders can falsify their weight by drinking water (up to 10 liters in one go in one documented case (Robinson, 2009)) or wearing weights or other objects…"

> "A 24-year-old female (BMI 11) on a general medical ward who, prior to a planned move

to an eating disorders unit, exercised by standing and wiggling her toes and fingers for the whole weekend, day and night, in front of two 'special nurses', before collapsing and dying from hypoglycemia on the Monday morning."

"A 19-year-old female patient (BMI 10) with renal failure on a medical ward who turned off her dextrose drip intended to rehydrate her and restore renal function, because having read the bottle she thought it had too many calories. She died within a few hours."

Another important fact is that there exists a correlation between high levels of stress and anxiety on the one hand and anorexia nervosa on the other. In my personal case, this comorbidity was, together with the drastic weight-loss, probably the most evident symptom.

Before developing anorexia, I was the happiest and most nonchalant person on earth. Nothing bothered me. I hardly knew what the word "stress" meant. I had no idea what it was like to feel anxiety; I never quarreled with anyone, never criticized or judged anyone; I was always content with my circumstances. In short, I lived and let live.

Once the disorder set in, however, I became more and more irritable, even aggressive, until my whole state of mind was characterized by a pervasive feeling of anxiety, of fear. I was always stressed, always in a hurry, always worried. I was so tense that I overreacted to all external stimuli. I was hypersensitive, touchy, quick-tempered. And very rapidly this irascible mood was to take a heavy toll on my relationships. People began to shun me, and I do not blame them. On the contrary, it still awes me how much patience and understanding some people showed towards me, for I was far from fun to be with!

Eating became the epitome of misery! Every meal was a condensed version of all the rituals I was compulsively performing. I preferred industrially processed products to homemade food because I could count the calories of the label. I always found a lame excuse to buy time — like the food being too hot, too cold, too salty, too sweet. I couldn't bear to see more than a minuscule quantity of food on my plate. I systematically had to rearrange the food before me, as if my life depended on getting the right angle between the squalid carrots and the lonesome cucumber facing one another on my plate. I chewed for hours until everyone around me lost their patience with me.

I also somehow often managed to have something extremely urgent to do precisely when it was time to sit at the table for a meal. My "headaches", "stomach pains", etc. would always mysteriously coincide with mealtimes.

I refused squarely to eat some foods like meat, fats, and oils. I lived permanently on a low-fat, low-carbohydrate diet — that is, until my self-control was overwhelmed by a bulimic craving for sweets, which happened with increasing frequency as I sunk into the disease. Then, all I would eat was desserts.

For days I felt an insatiable desire, bordering on addiction, for certain sweets. In particular, I was so obsessed with a specific kind of palm-shaped cake covered with chocolate glazing that I'd do whatever it took to get one. I still remember with a shiver the many hours of my life I squandered, slavishly obeying the compulsion to satisfy my craving. After a long day's fasting, I would go out in the middle of the night desperately chasing after those specific cakes, sometimes for hours, until I found one to my liking.

Sometimes I ate less in a whole day than what is now half of my breakfast, and every time I'd finally eat something I'd become consumed by guilt.

I was permanently hungry — hungry in the morning, hungry in the afternoon, and, by the time evening came, starving.

When going to sleep I was so hungry that almost every night I dreamt I was finally eating real food, like fish or meat. So vivid was the appearance, smell, and taste of the food, that I spent most of my nights actually *gnawing* that hallucination. And since I had nothing to chew but a delusion, I was spending my nights uncontrollably grinding my teeth, which soon caused premature tooth wear, mandibular joint dysfunction, and permanent neck pain. Later on, I learned that this condition is called bruxism.

I still look back in amazement at the apparent physical stamina I had during the disorder, even in the worst years. I cannot figure out where my emaciated body — all just skin and bones — could manage to hold any energy!

Without going into too much detail about the physiological processes brought about by the disorder, the most visible sign of depletion was that once all the fat was gone, my body started to seek energy elsewhere, which eventually led to the cannibalistic consumption of its own muscle and bone tissue over the years — and, sadly enough, a good part of it was never to come back.

Some days I was so weak that I just fainted, especially in the last stages of the disorder, but even then I had the audacity to try to justify those fits by putting the blame on my naturally occurring bradycardia and very low blood pressure. A bad excuse is better than none!

Like most anorexics, I lived in a permanent state of hypothermia due to not having enough energy available to support all the body's vital functions. It was just like I'd fallen into freezing water, but with the difference that mine was not an accidental or short exposure, but a deliberate and permanent one.

The whole world had become a cold place for me; I felt like I was living in a refrigerated cell, while everybody else was enjoying the warm weather. Towards the end, things got worse, and I became a cold-blooded reptile: I spent most of my days chasing the sun, like a lizard. I could literally spend whole days sitting under the sun on a park bench, trying to warm up my scrawny body, which by then was incapable of keeping its own temperature stable at a biologically fit level without external assistance.

My body had to make do with the little energy available and tried to protect the vital organs inside, so it shut the bloodstream to the peripheral muscles, mostly feet and hands, to protect the core. Despite the mildness of the climate where I lived, as a result of years of severe deprivation, in the final stages of the disorder my hands — evidently the last in line for blood supply — were so full of frostbite blisters and so grey in color that my friends kept telling me that I could play the role of a zombie in a horror movie...without any make-up. And they were right!

I remember that once I had to go to the local hospital in a cold winter's day, and upon admission, the nurse asked me what happened to my hands and put a monitoring device on one of my fingers. Presently, seeing that the reading of the results was abnormal, she thought something was wrong with that particular device, and went to get another one from another section, only to realize that the new one showed the same result. Both devices were functioning correctly: my hands were not.

On that cold morning, my fingers were lifeless, but even by milder weather, my fingers were an appalling sight: they were full of open wounds, crimson scars, and mostly uncovered nailbeds. I was diagnosed with secondary Raynaud's syndrome, from which I never completely recovered: still today, more than twenty years later, I have to live with this limiting condition.

Every time I have to treat my frostbite blisters in the

winter I cannot help but think about all the damage that anorexics inflict upon themselves. I also now regard the scars in my fingers as a constant lesson of the past. Whereas some people have positive affirmations tattooed on their skins to remind them how to live, I have scars on my fingers tattooed by the disease as a permanent reminder of how not to live. And although I cannot change the past, I can learn from it and share my experience with the world so that others do not have to endure the same suffering as I did.

I could go on describing the fanatic rituals which my life had been reduced to, stuff that still today, twenty years later, makes me feel deeply ashamed of myself: I had become a slave of my own obsessive mind.

Every hour, every minute, every second of my wretched life was occupied by the disorder: nothing else mattered anymore. Family, friends, love, fun... and even myself: everything was subordinate to the illness.

I lost all interest in anything which was not directly related to serving the objectives of my anorexic mind. Everything I liked before, all that I enjoyed so much doing — riding my mountain-bike, surfing, fishing, snorkeling, reading books, writing — in short, all those little things that made me happy day by day faded in the haze of my obsession.

I even lost all interest in sex, which had been, and later, after my recovery, again became an essential part of my life. It is interesting to note that sex and writing disappeared from my life at the same time: both are creative activities that require energy and bring about growth. And we can only create and grow when we are not in "protection mode", because when we are, our sympathetic nervous system directs our available energy to short-term life-preserving functions, at the expense of growth, creation, and procreation. When you're anorexic, you live constantly under a perceived threat — while the only actual threat is your eating disorder itself. You're in a permanent state of survival in which growth is impossible.

No sex, no fun, no creation, no life, only self-destruction. Anorexia was my boss, and I was its servant. I was no longer free, I was not living an independent life, let alone a happy life.

Indeed, I had *no life at all*.

Physical Decline

MATTHEW 6:22-23[9]

When you're anorexic, your whole self-perception is distorted by the disorder. What you actually look like is of no importance, in fact, you are not even aware of your real aspect: you only see what *you think* you look like. For five long years, I was unable to see myself: I looked in the mirror and I only saw what my anorexic mind wanted me to see.

Although the selective perception of reality is a constant trait of our interaction with the world, this inherent partiality of the mind is exacerbated by mental disorders. We all live according to our own interpretation of reality, but certain mental conditions increase the vividness of these visions until they become real. Our whole life reflects our subjective thoughts, and so, our subjective experience carries more power than our objective situation. We always create our own reality.

What was then the reality that I was unable to see in the mirror? What did I actually look like? When my anorexia began, I was 175 cm tall (about 5'9") and weighed 70 kg (about 154 lbs.), and I had a lean and muscular body, with an average body mass index, or BMI, of 22.

At the lowest point of my disorder, my BMI dropped to 16. I weighed only 49 kg for almost the same height. I say "almost" because not only did I look smaller due to my inability to stand upright, but I *actually* lost some height due to muscular atrophy and osteopenia.

Before developing anorexia, I used to have white teeth, strong nails, thick hair, and a healthy-looking suntanned skin. After only two years living with the disease, my whole body was emaciated and lifeless. My teeth looked unhealthy and my nails were brittle. I'd lost a lot of hair, and what remained was dull and sparse.

If I had to choose only one color to describe my whole appearance, it would be yellow. I was yellow all over, partly due to carotenoderma induced by excessive carrot consumption. My skin was yellow, my eyeballs were yellow, my teeth were yellow, my nails were yellow, and even my tongue was yellow — definitely not the body of a young male in the prime of life.

Every time I see pictures now from that period I shudder at the sight of that heap of skin and bone I had become. But could I see my real aspect then at all? Far from it! I saw myself as being completely normal, even on the plump side, totally blind to my pathetic appearance.

This is very important to understand, because the first question that probably comes to your mind every time you see a picture of someone afflicted by anorexia is: why are they doing this, can't they see themselves?

I, for one, could not. And I dare believe that most anorexics are totally unaware of their frightful, even revolting, appearance — and this is one of the reasons that make anorexia one of the most difficult mental disorders to treat. Not only do they resist, or even refuse, treatment, but most do not even accept that something might be wrong with them.

Treatment Unwanted, Dead or Alive

Patients with anorexia nervosa are subject to an extreme compulsion to pursue thinness. This compulsion has been likened to addiction to heroin and patients will take terrible risks in order to satisfy it. (...) The patient should be regarded as being under an irresistible compulsion and, unless their mental state changes, they are powerless to alter their behavior.

MARSIPAN report[8]

The mental processes which lead patients to shun treatment can be extremely intricate: from the basic fear of getting fat to more complex processes, such as a distorted reaction to certain external stimuli (pictures of overweight vs. thin people, images of food, etc.); an altered brain response to new habits, which creates an insurmountable aversion to any kind of change in diet or in the rituals they perform every day; or a persevering determination to show their superiority by carrying out a supposedly personal decision.

Recent studies have also shown that anorexic patients have an increased capacity to delay reward and thus stick relentlessly to the long-term objective of losing weight — which makes them steadfast in their determination to achieve this goal.

However, the ultimate cause of the refusal to admit the problem is to be found in the total obfuscation of the mind brought about by the disorder.

My case was a combination of all the above factors, with the result that I didn't want to be healed in the first place. When encouraged to gain weight, not only did I feel extremely anxious about my physical appearance, but also restricted in my freedom to achieve my goal. First, because I associated my healing from the disorder with becoming fat — even though I had never been overweight before developing anorexia; and second, because I identified "healing" with "defeat" (i.e. the inability to carry my plan to a conclusion).

My mind bombarded me with thoughts relentlessly, such as: "don't trust them, you look swell! They'll never be able to do what you have done, they are just envious of your success. You're past master at self-control...", and I thought I was, like Kafka's hunger artist, but what I could not see was that I was playing in the wrong league. A pathetic reality lay underneath the protective shell of personal accomplishment and victory created by my mind: I had been defeated by the disorder. I was just a loser.

The harsh truth was that deep down I felt a paralyzing fear that led to uncontrollable — and often humiliating — obsessive behaviors, such as lying about what I'd eaten, concealing food, ingesting laxatives, vomiting, and exercising compulsively.

Anorexia rapidly creates a vicious circle of fasting and obsession. The less you eat, the more you weaken your nervous system by depriving it of essential nutrients, and this, in turn, increases the vulnerability of that very same system to negative external stimuli.

You soon develop an emotional hypersensitivity that can easily lead to fanaticism. You lose all sense of proportion and end up overreacting to anything that would otherwise not affect you.

In other words, by starving and weakening your nervous system you're feeding and strengthening your anorexia. And so it goes on and on until you reach a state of total physical breakdown.

To make things worse, most people suffering from anorexia only seek treatment when they are already in the final stages of the disease, usually taken to hospital by a relative, with visible signs of physical collapse, which can be already too late, because most patients with anorexia seem to be misleadingly well, even very energetic right up to a fatal physical failure.

The reason for this is that anorexia is just like a psychotropic drug that controls your mind, and, since your mind controls your body, the latter blindly obeys the commands of your anorexic brain, which will do *whatever it takes* to burn more and more calories.

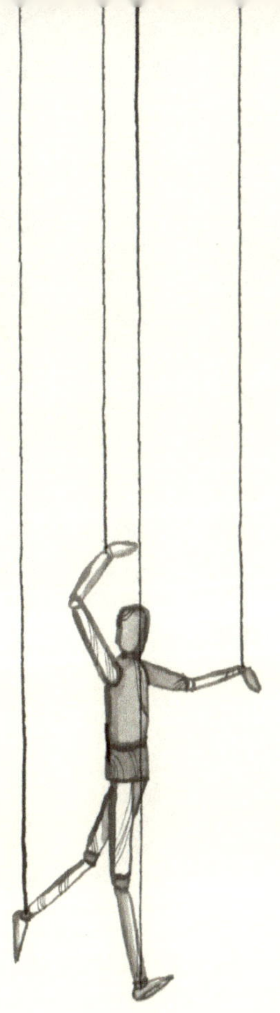

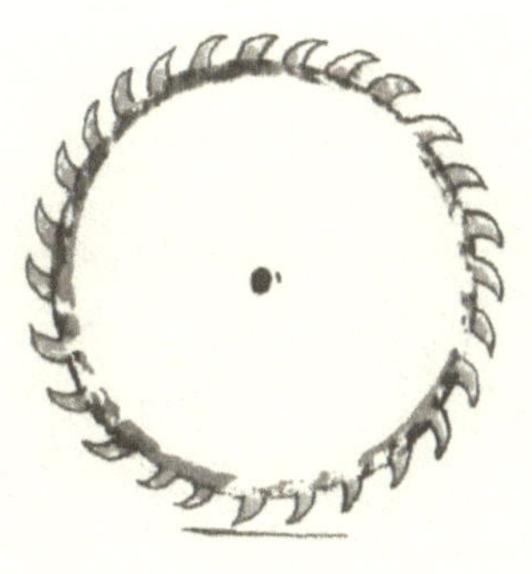

PART · II

How I survived my mind
- The disk repair tool

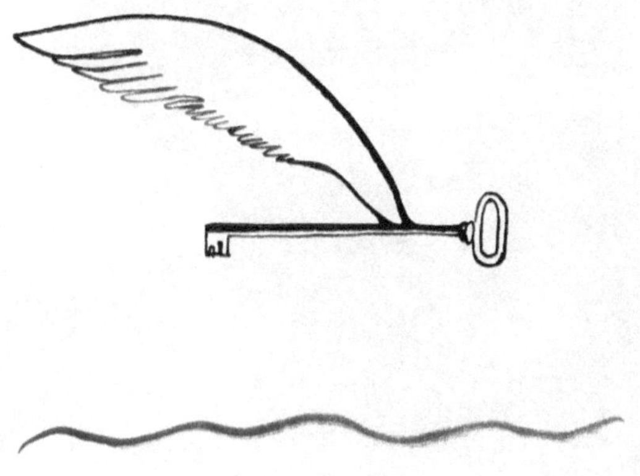

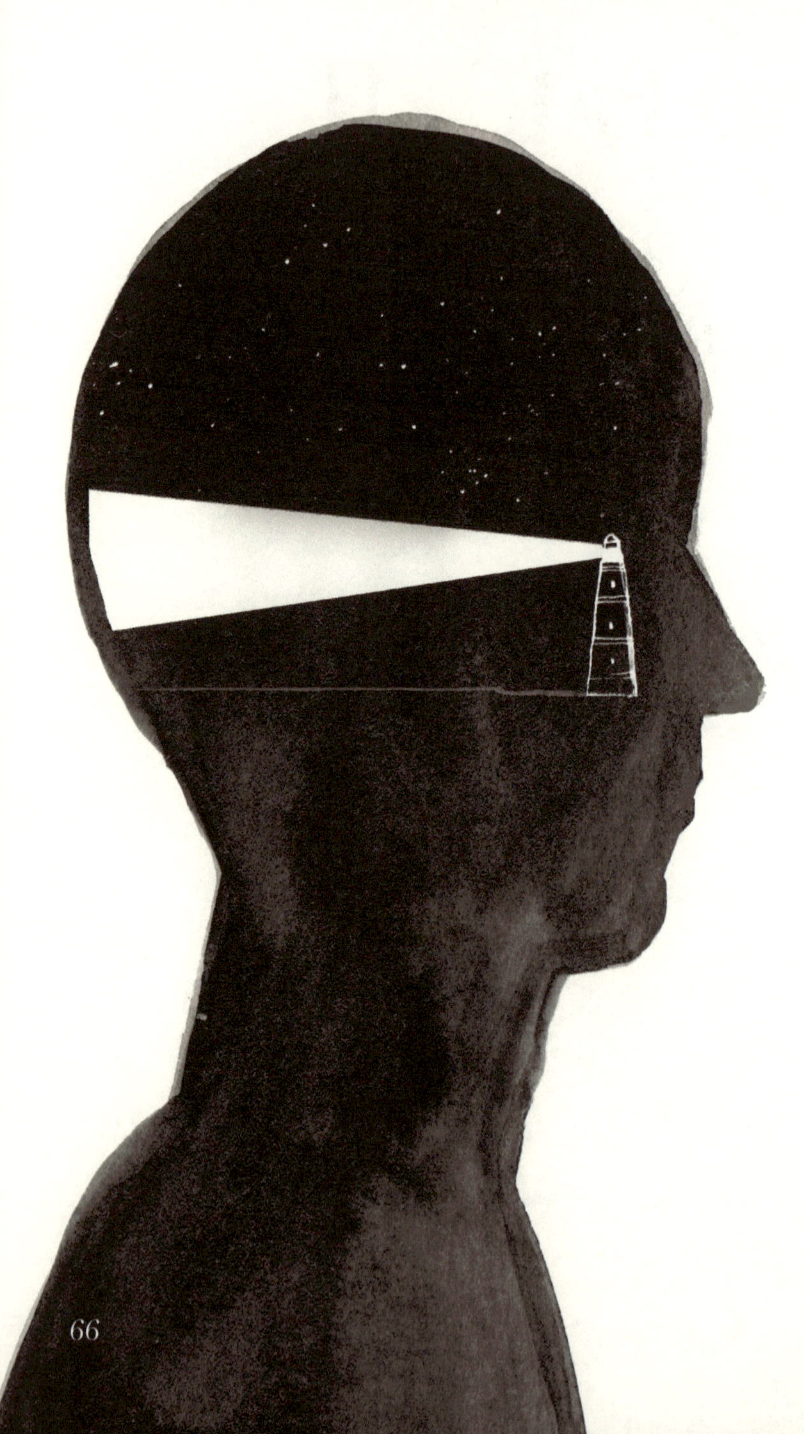

If a diver is to secure pearls he must descend to the bottom of the sea, braving all dangers of jagged coral and vicious sharks. So man must face the perils of worldly passion if he is to secure the precious pearl of Enlightenment. He must first be lost among the mountainous crags of egoism and selfishness, before there will awaken in him the desire to find a path that will lead him to Enlightenment.

From *The Teaching of Buddha*[3]

ON THE ROPES

The mind is its own place, and in itself
can make a heaven of hell, a hell of heaven.
JOHN MILTON, *Paradise Lost*[10]

We don't see with our eyes, we see with our minds, and, in my mind, I still saw myself as being physically healthy and mentally strong. That was my reality, the only one that existed for me, but that was not the frightening reality that the rest of the world could see. By then I was reduced to a feeble walking skeleton, a bi-dimensional creepy yellow zombie who was not even able to walk straight. Everybody could see it then, and everybody *did* see it. Everybody but me! My mind had created its own separate reality which contradicted all the external messages and warnings I was receiving. Only much later, when I hit rock bottom, did I begin to recognize that something was going wrong, that

I was not normal anymore. Hard to believe that it took me so long!

As the disorder began to be so obvious that everybody could see it, the social pressure around me grew until it became unbearable. I ultimately gave in to the constant requests of friends and family, and reluctantly accepted to seek professional help — not because I believed I needed it, for I would still not even *acknowledge* that I had anorexia, let alone admit that I needed help — but simply to do them a favor.

Indeed, most people with anorexia only begin to acknowledge their disease, and their actual physical appearance, when they reach such a state of physical depletion that they have to be taken to hospital lest they die... and some of them will eventually die even under medical care. Sadly, too many anorexic patients die from the physical consequences of the disorder, and most survivors never recover completely. I consider it a miracle that I'm still alive today, and almost totally recovered.

Like many anorexics, I too refused to cooperate with the few doctors I accepted to visit. I had no real desire to recover because I didn't see that there was anything to recover from. I stealthily sabotaged all their attempts to cure me. In the beginning, I resorted to noncooperation, which then degenerated into outright hostility that translated into me becoming a compulsive liar.

The doctors eventually said that as long as I did not acknowledge that I had a severe eating disorder, and accept to cooperate with them, there was nothing they could do. And there the treatment ended.

How was I on my own going to change my reality and control my mind, the very part of me that was controlling me?

Trying to overpower my anorexic mind was like trying to stop a tsunami while being just a drop in that huge mass of water, and now I know that I would not have been able to overcome the disorder without external help. And the help finally came … in a most extraordinary way.

Here's how it happened.

Introducing the Ultimate Doctor: G. Reaper

*Though thou shouldest be going to live three thousand years,
and as many times ten thousand years, still remember that no
man loses any other life than this which he now lives,
nor lives any other than this which he now loses.*

Marcus Aurelius, *Meditations*[11]

I started surfing as a 10-year-old, and for more than twelve years, right up to the onset of my eating disorder, surfing was the activity I enjoyed most in life. My daily surfing session was the center of gravity around which orbited my whole reality. The first thing I did every day was to look out the window, check the waves, and plan my day according to the conditions and the tide.

I was extremely lucky to grow up right in front of a beach. Every day I could see from my window the vast Atlantic Ocean disappearing in the horizon, follow the tides, and watch the swell. I lived so close to the ocean that I only had to cross the street, walk down to the beach in my wetsuit, and jump into the water.

At the beginning of my anorexic decline, I continued surfing as usual and enjoying it, although my head had already started to be in a different place. The surfing didn't feel as good as it used to, but I didn't attribute any particular significance to this. However, I gradually lost interest in it.

Later on, when I had no more body fat to protect me, the wetsuits that had kept me warm in the past were now unable to maintain my body temperature at a comfortable level. As a result, I eventually stopped riding waves altogether, which was the very last thing that I still enjoyed doing. I thus buried the last beacon of hope in my life, and put the seal on my own death sentence.

It is ironic that it was precisely surfing, which used to be my life, that would one day almost kill me. I had to literally touch rock bottom to wake up, and it all happened on one cold November day.

In the fall of 1998, I was at the lowest point of my disorder: I felt disoriented in the maze of my own mind. I was sinking deeper and deeper into desperation, into hopelessness, drowning in the toxic pond of my obsessions. Dark thoughts came to fill the inner emptiness of the last months, transforming the pointless void into destructive nihilism.

Life had lost its meaning, and, for the first time, I

began to consider putting an end to my suffering.

The certainty of death had inevitably become more attractive than the unbearable uncertainty of a meaningless life, and yet, I still held on to mine... but for how long? I realized that my only salvation would be in finding a meaning for my existence, a reason not to die, so I spent hours every day frantically walking alone in forsaken thorny tracks along the rugged Atlantic coast, trying to find an aim for my aimless life, aside from the pathetic goal of becoming the thinnest man on Earth.

One morning I felt like strolling along the sand. It was a misty winter's day, the swell was good, and the surf fairly big, breaking far away from the shore. I stood there staring in the cold breeze, paralyzed by the mighty roar of the waves dissolving into a ghostly haze as they crashed on the shore.

Suddenly, I felt a powerful urge to ride those waves, as if inside of me there was an irresistible force pushing me to jump into the water.

I started to experience once again that joyful sense of purpose which had totally disappeared from my life: it was the first time in months that I really *wanted to do something different* from fasting.

I decided to drive to a deserted beach that I particularly liked, where I would be alone, and also find better waves. I hurried back home, grabbed my surfboard and wetsuit, and drove to the beach.

The surfing conditions were not ideal, however. Although the waves were just as big as I had expected, a powerful onshore wind caused them to close in random sections, and the tide was already ebbing out, forming strong rip currents which cut through the line of breaking waves like rivers flowing out to sea.

It took me a long time to paddle in: the bar was far from the shore, and I had to fight my way to get there, ducking a thousand times under the broken waves that were rolling towards the beach. Under normal circumstances, I would have given up as soon as I saw the real conditions, but my life was no longer normal.

However, as soon as I left the bar behind and made it to the point break, I began to enjoy the ride. My mind was totally *present* in the now. I was once again savoring life without wondering why, or thinking about what would happen next. I took profound delight just in being out there in the ocean on my own, drifting on my surfboard, and feeling the cold wind against my face.

I eventually caught and rode two or three waves, which I enjoyed thoroughly, but being out of practice I also missed many others. In the end, after missing some series, I paddled like a madman to catch a big wave, caught it, stood up, and started on a vertical takeoff down the wall to take a bottom turn. That's when I lost balance and fell.

"Just another wipe-out", I thought to myself. In the past twelve years, I had ridden thousands of waves and fallen a zillion times, so why would a zillion plus one make any difference? As soon as I fell off the surfboard, the wave hit me, sucked me under the water, rolled me like a washing machine, pushed me down to the seabed, and kept me there. Again, I knew that familiar feeling, and I didn't panic.

Fighting against a wave is counterproductive. Waves are much stronger than us, and in fighting them we consume more oxygen. So, it's wiser to relax and keep calm, let the wave pass, and then swim up to the surface once the pressure of the water has subsided.

But this time something was different. Not only did I feel calm down there in the darkness, but a pleasant sensation of profound stillness filled my mind with joy, with a beautiful inner peace I hadn't known for so long that I'd almost forgotten how good it was. Now, for the first time in years, something stopped the ruthless mechanical clockwork of my obsessive anorexic mind, and there was silence inside.

So good did it feel that I suddenly felt no urge whatsoever to reach the surface and breathe again. I was enjoying this newly found inner peace and did not think about *anything at all*, let alone about swimming back to the hopelessness of an existence of chaos and pain. All I really wanted was to prolong as much as possible that wonderful feeling of serenity.

I decided to give up the fight for life. In fact, there was nothing left to fight for. I had tried for so many years that it seemed a lifetime, but now I felt exhausted, and I did not have either the strength or the will to go on. I could no longer deny that I had been defeated by the disorder, that my own life had long become secondary in value compared to my obsession. Dying was just the price I had to pay in exchange for the bliss of a peaceful mind.

Then something happened, something hard to describe. I felt a huge blow, as if something big and powerful had hit me and knocked me out. I opened my eyes — or I think I did — and saw a large dark object drifting under the water, only to realize in fright that it was my own body and that I was standing outside of it, watching the whole scene. All was quiet as if time had stopped — just like in a dream.

I don't know how long I spent observing this object,

my own physical self, but it seemed an eternity. Suddenly the peaceful sensation that I'd been enjoying so much vanished. All I could feel was a mixture of hatred and pity: I despised what I saw drifting there under the water.

Then there was only darkness and silence.

The next thing I remember is an excruciating pain in my chest, and my whole body shaken by a racking cough. I was now floating on the surface of the water.

At first, the idea that I could still survive did not provoke any reaction from my depleted body. Instead of actively trying to save my life, I just drifted. I still couldn't see any reason to continue living, and I felt too weak to do anything other than close my eyes and wait for the next wave to suck me down under the water again.

Then everything around me evanesced as I sunk deep into the darkness for the second time.

I don't remember what happened next, nor for how long, but I began to feel a relentless force taking command of my muscles, literally forcing my limbs to move, to pull my surfboard by the leash, and to hold on to it.

It was as if a power that had been dormant inside

had just been activated, as if an ignition key had suddenly started an unknown engine, which made me swim and fight for my life.

I held on to my surfboard and was eventually washed ashore. Frozen and exhausted, I crawled out of the water and dragged myself onto the wet sand. I remember how I lay there on the beach, holding my knees to my chest, curled up like a fetus, coughing wildly, and vomiting water.

I remained in that position until I was able to slowly move again, stretch my body, and sit up. At first, it was like waking up with relief from a long nightmare, but the relief waned rapidly under the pressure of an overwhelming feeling of anger, frustration, and shame. The awakening brought about the inescapable awareness of what I had done to myself: horrible images began to appear in my mind, first slowly, then more and more rapidly, until everything around me became a macabre kaleidoscope of shameful visions of self-annihilation. I was violently teleported into the apocalyptic helter-skelter of cruel punishments in Hieronymus Bosch's "Last Judgement", where vicious red demons and anthropomorphous beasts ruthlessly savaged countless clones of my naked body in hundreds of simultaneous scenes; a glimpse of the eternal nemesis in which we are both victims and executioners, for in the countenance of each fiendish tormentor I saw no other face than my own.

I don't know how long I sat there. Ten minutes? Ten hours? All my attention was drawn to the eerie parade of visions of my life that were spinning around me. I was sitting there in a mysterious movie theater, watching the film of my own life. It was a profoundly unsettling feeling. I sympathized with the main character, I wanted to talk to him, to help him stop his ruthless self-destruction, but I couldn't. I had to watch the full movie like an unwilling voyeur, and witness my own torture, my own obliteration.

Then the film ended abruptly. The visions stopped moving and a static image appeared.

I saw myself in the present moment, not the distorted image that had for so long sneered at me from the mirror, but my real self at last — and what I saw made me feel so sorry for that forlorn character that suddenly all the hatred and anger vanished. I had to face what was left of myself: sitting on that beach was the ghost of the person I once had been. I was a wreck, a monstrous skeleton among windswept dunes on a deserted beach.

At that moment, I was looking at my starved body as a loving father looks at his newborn child:

without any judgment, aware of its fragility, but full of expectation for the new life ahead.

Then I stared motionlessly at the roaring waves pounding on the shore under the gloomy overcast sky, reflecting on everything I had endured until I could no longer bear it, and then I burst: I started to scream as loud as I could. I screamed again and again in the barren solitude of the vacant beach until I had no more voice left, but the only reply was the piercing laughter of the waves riding on the breeze.

Then I began to cry. The salt of my tears joined the salt of the drops of seawater as they fell down my face. I cried as I'd never cried before — moved by a mixture of vile feelings of regret and self-pity, and lofty hopes of self-forgiveness and recovery.

The subtle, but unequivocal promise of a new existence shone dimly in the distance, like a waning rainbow over the horizon of my wretched life. Albeit subdued, those were the first rays of light in my darkness, the first colors in my gloomy life.

I saw there the end of a cruel journey of self-destruction — the nadir of decline and the beginning of growth. On the outside I was still no more than a living corpse; but inside, something had changed. Changed radically. Something was fighting for a new life.

I didn't yet know why I felt so different, but I knew I did. Only later, when flashbacks of what I'd gone through under the water started to haunt me, did I realize how life-changing that experience had been.

For years I was totally under the control of the disorder, so only a huge shock could knock me out of my pathetic fictional world of counting and burning calories at all costs, and bring me back to reality. In my case, that shock came in the form of a traumatic experience. The sight of my own demise had pierced through my body like a fork of lightning, an electroshock that woke me up from my nightmare.

What exactly happened inside while I was under the water is hard to convey. It was definitely not something that came out of a state of consciousness — it came from a far deeper place. Something within, more powerful than my own will, made me fight to live, and that something was the unconscious activation of the dormant, but powerful survival instinct that resides in the unfathomable depths of every living creature, our last resort to maintain this mystery we call life.

In a life-threatening situation, when our repressive conscious mind is no longer powerful enough to subdue it, this instinct will do whatever it takes to achieve the self-preservation of the being, and thus the survival of the body in which it lives. This most primeval of all our instincts superseded what was left of my will, and took command of my body, forcing me to swim up to the surface and grab hold of my surfboard.

In the presence of Death, the great equalizer, all the goals dictated by the anorexic obsessions which had controlled my life for the last years became meaningless — it was like coming back to reality from an eerie dream; only the self-imposed suffering was still real then. I realized with shame that I had been on the verge of destroying the most beautiful gift I had: my life.

Mors ultima linea rerum (death is the ultimate boundary of things): crossing the last line to the place of no return meant the end of suffering, but also the end of all experience — the end of love, the end of happiness, the end of creation. It meant the end of this wonderful journey that we call life, prematurely aborted by purposeless wanton self-destruction.

On that beach, I surrendered to the will of a force much greater than me, a force that wanted me to live, and twenty years later I can confidently say that that was the moment my new life began. I had been given a second chance, and although I didn't know why I had deserved it, I knew that it was the last.

Now my life was in my hands only, and I realized that if I was to survive at all, I could never be the same again. I had to start anew. I must either rise or die.

Awake, arise or be forever fallen.
JOHN MILTON, *Paradise Lost*[10]

Love for Death, Lust for Life

Where death waits for us is uncertain; let us look
for him everywhere. The premeditation of death is
the premeditation of liberty; he who has learned to
die has unlearned to serve.

MICHEL DE MONTAIGNE, *Essays*[2]

I got home on the verge of serious hypothermia. Observing my wasted body in the bathroom mirror, I recognized the same corpse that I'd seen earlier on. And yet, something was different. My eyes had a totally new expression. There was new strength in my sight — an almost manic determination that I'd never seen there before.

After all the self-inflicted suffering that I had endured, my near-death experience activated what the early philosophies of psychology and metaphysics called "conatus", or the innate inclination of a thing to continue to exist and enhance itself: an inexorable will to live and thrive.

That day, a new life began for me, and with it, a long and painful process of recovery. I had no idea what I was going to do with my life, but I had the will to do whatever it took to be myself, to resuscitate the child that I once was. It was the beginning of happiness. I felt reborn.

I took a long shower and enjoyed the sensation of the hot water running along my freezing skin. It was good, and for the first time in years, I was able to resist the temptation of turning off the hot water to stand under the cold shower, as I'd done almost every day since the disorder began, just to burn more of the non-existent fat from my body. And this apparently unimportant event was, in fact, the first and greatest lesson in my new life: I had to stop suffering and start enjoying the small pleasures of life.

This lesson changed radically my idea of happiness. I realized that a state of permanent bliss cannot be a distant lofty goal, an unattainable dream, but must be the sum total of every single moment of bliss in our lives, insignificant as they may seem at first sight. And since happiness can only be enjoyed in life, in *this* life, and since the only real manifestation of our life at any moment can exclusively take place in the present, if we manage to transform every present moment of our existence into a happy one, our entire life will be happy.

While I was still enjoying the shower, I got the distinct feeling that I was not alone, that there was somebody else in that bathroom. And I knew who it was.

I had met her a while ago on the beach, and I could still perceive her presence, now closer than ever; so close that I felt her cold breath on my neck. I overcame my fear and suddenly turned around expecting to see a frightening sight, but I just saw water, running down the tiled wall — and yet, I *knew* she was there. Although I couldn't see her, Death was definitely there, not as a mere reminiscence of what had happened earlier on that day, but as a tangible presence that filled the entire room.

The fear was soon replaced by acceptance, for I quickly surrendered to the inevitability of her presence: I saw there was nothing I could do if she wanted to be around, so I might as well get used to her company. Anyway, for all I knew, I should have been dead by now, so every additional minute of life had become a gift. I realized that I had to almost die to start living, and this made me feel a deep sense of love and gratitude, mixed with an almost erotic feeling of intimacy. I was deeply indebted to her, for I knew well that she was the all-powerful exorcist who had chased the devil out of my mind. I did not want her to go away, and I guess my inner feelings could be felt by her, for she was evidently not in any hurry to leave my side.

Even today, she's always around me — my faithful companion. And her very presence is what makes every moment of my life so unique, so special, but also so fleeting.

Death is the antagonistic power that makes life so valuable. The magic of life stems from its finiteness, and the imminence of death is what makes your time so precious.

I realized that life is just like a butterfly on a flower: we must enjoy it while we can because it will soon fly away, never to return.

Every day, when I wake up, Death reminds me that it may be my last — she whispers into my ear that although I'm now watching the sun rise, I might not get to see it set. Her presence is a constant reminder of the precious value of every second, every minute, every hour of our existence.

On that November day, I decided to stop taking life for granted. Still in the presence of Death, I made

the firm commitment to enjoy everything in my
life, to live every moment of my new life as fully as
I can — and I have stuck to that commitment ever
since.

94

To the guests that must go bid God's speed
and brush away all traces of their steps.
Take to your bosom with a smile
what is easy and simple and near.
Today is the festival of phantoms
that know not when they die.
Let your laughter be but a meaningless mirth
like twinkles of light on the ripples.
Let your life lightly dance on the edges of Time
like dew on the tip of a leaf.
Strike in chords from your harp fitful momentary rhythms.

RABINDRANATH TAGORE, *The gardener*[12]

Stairway to Heaven

The well-known phrase "fall seven times, stand up eight" is a good description of my long, hard journey toward recovery. I fell a thousand times, but I knew I had to get up and keep on fighting, because now I had a purpose to live for, and an infinite lust for life and happiness.

In the days that followed, I made a number of decisions to change my life. The first one was to fight this battle on my own. I knew from experience that no help from my family or social environment could make me change, at least not yet. Consequently, not only did I keep to myself what had happened on that extraordinary day, but I made the firm promise not to let anyone know that I had decided to recover from my anorexia.

In fact, I kept that promise so well that I never told anyone about the events of that day — until now, with this book. The recent suicide of three people I knew well, together with the silent emotional distress in which I realized that many people around me are living — people who seem to have everything — were compelling enough reasons to let that dormant seed grow, and blossom into a book.

Of the many things that I learned from my father when I was a child, three precepts of his still stand out like islands in an ocean of wisdom: "Never complain, never explain, and never tell anyone about your plans". I saw in the reintroduction of these three rules into my life the first step towards recovery.

On the practical side, I started my cure by introducing a routine of *affirmations* about my new self. I knew that if I ever was to change my external situation, I first had to change internally. Every day my first thought was concentrated on my main objective: "regain my health and build up my body". I would even write it down every morning in my diary as the first and most important task of the day, right after waking up, and I also used to carry in my pocket a piece of cardboard in which I'd written the same phrase on one side and "I choose to be happy" on the other.

I needed this constant self-suggestion to help me face all the adversities along the road to recovery, and it had to be a material reminder, something I could hold in my hands, feel in my pocket, and read again and again.

I also realized that I needed solitude, silence, and new surroundings, so I decided to leave home after Christmas to go to Paris. Even though I was perfectly aware that all the problems were inside, I also knew that external change can contribute to internal transformation. Having traveled all my life, I knew well the feeling of "leaving the problems behind" that we experience when we hit the road. Superficial as this kind of change may be, it still helps in that it frees you from many local constraints that can act as obstacles to your new life.

Solitude sometimes is best society
John Milton, Paradise Lost[10]

Then came the hardest part, at least physically —
starting to eat normally. It took me several weeks
just to control my aversion to food. I needed to
convince myself that food was not just necessary,
but good, and that no food could do me more harm
than my eating disorder did. Above all, I had to stop
seeing any weight gain as a personal defeat.

It was not easy. For weeks my body refused the
extra food. The sight of more and richer food than
usual on my dish was enough to trigger my aversion
and make me feel sick. I often felt like throwing up,
even before starting to eat, but I could not see any
other way ahead than to keep on trying, slowly, but
persistently.

Sometimes it was so hard that I considered taking
the easy way out and giving up, but my love for
life had now become too strong to accept defeat.
So, in spite of all obstacles, I persevered, and that
perseverance made me stronger day by day. After a
while, I got so used to facing setbacks that I soon
developed the resilience of a punching-ball: the
harder I was pushed down, the faster I sprung back,
and the tougher I was hit, the stronger I bounced
back.

Like those work-hardened metals that are
strengthened by deformation and strain, I too

learned to grow tougher under pressure.

Then one day a miracle happened. I sat down to eat a meal and my body not only accepted it, but appeared to want more. I became so happy that I ate as much as I could. The nightmare is finally over, I thought. But soon after the meal, I felt unwell and vomited. The huge difference was, however, that now it was neither self-induced vomiting, nor caused by binge-eating, and that made the whole difference: I just had gone too fast for what my atrophied stomach could cope with in one go.

Despite losing that first minor battle, the mere fact of being able to accept food without fear was a great feeling. Just like for a mountaineer the summit-snack — no matter how frugal — becomes the most delicious treat in the world, food never tasted so good as it did during those first months of my recovery.

I was making progress and I knew then that I would win the battle. I had accomplished the most fundamental step: I had recovered my ability to master my obsessive thoughts, to conquer compulsive behaviors. After so many years of being controlled by an anorexic mind, now it was I who was in control. And since it was clear to me that my mind was cured, my body would necessarily follow.

It was just a matter of perseverance.

That awareness was the real beginning of the long story of my physical recovery from anorexia: a story of battles lost and won; a story of carefully reeducating my body to eat; a story of literally spoon-feeding myself as if I was a newborn baby; a story of fighting against my deepest fears; a story of new hope as my nails and hair started to grow healthy again… a story that still goes on.

Even today, when I consider myself to be almost totally recovered, sometimes I find myself entertaining useless and treacherous thoughts about food. However, the huge difference between now and the past is that I have learned to identify and control any attempt of my mind to wander off track and get lost in the perilous jungle of pathological obsessions.

My initial estimate of the actual length of the recovery process was somewhat optimistic, though. Not only did the recovery take years, but it is still unfinished as I write these lines today, more than two decades later. However, I realized soon enough that neither the duration nor even the accomplishment of the healing was as important as the little victories won every day, because time passes regardless of what we do with it, so making the most of it in the present is what really matters.

As long as we are doing the right thing in the present, and thoroughly enjoying it, we have reached our goal for today. And today is the only reality we have, for the past and the future exist only in our mind, in the form of memories and expectations. Our entire life is condensed in one everlasting moment called now, and if that moment is filled with joy, our whole life will be, for what is life but the succession of those present moments?

Hard as it was, all along the way I was positively aware that every day I was fulfilling the two promises that I always carried with me in my pocket, and that was enough to keep fighting. Besides, in life the real challenge is not so much to try to heal at all costs our physical and emotional wounds — lest the very healing process become a new obsession — but to learn to live unapologetically with our scars, accept our past, forgive ourselves, and keep on going forward.

Never underestimate the power of your mind. Believe in your ability to create your own reality, for if you do, every day is going to be just better than the previous one — you will make it better!

Let this belief be your *why*. When you have the *why*, you will always find the *how*.

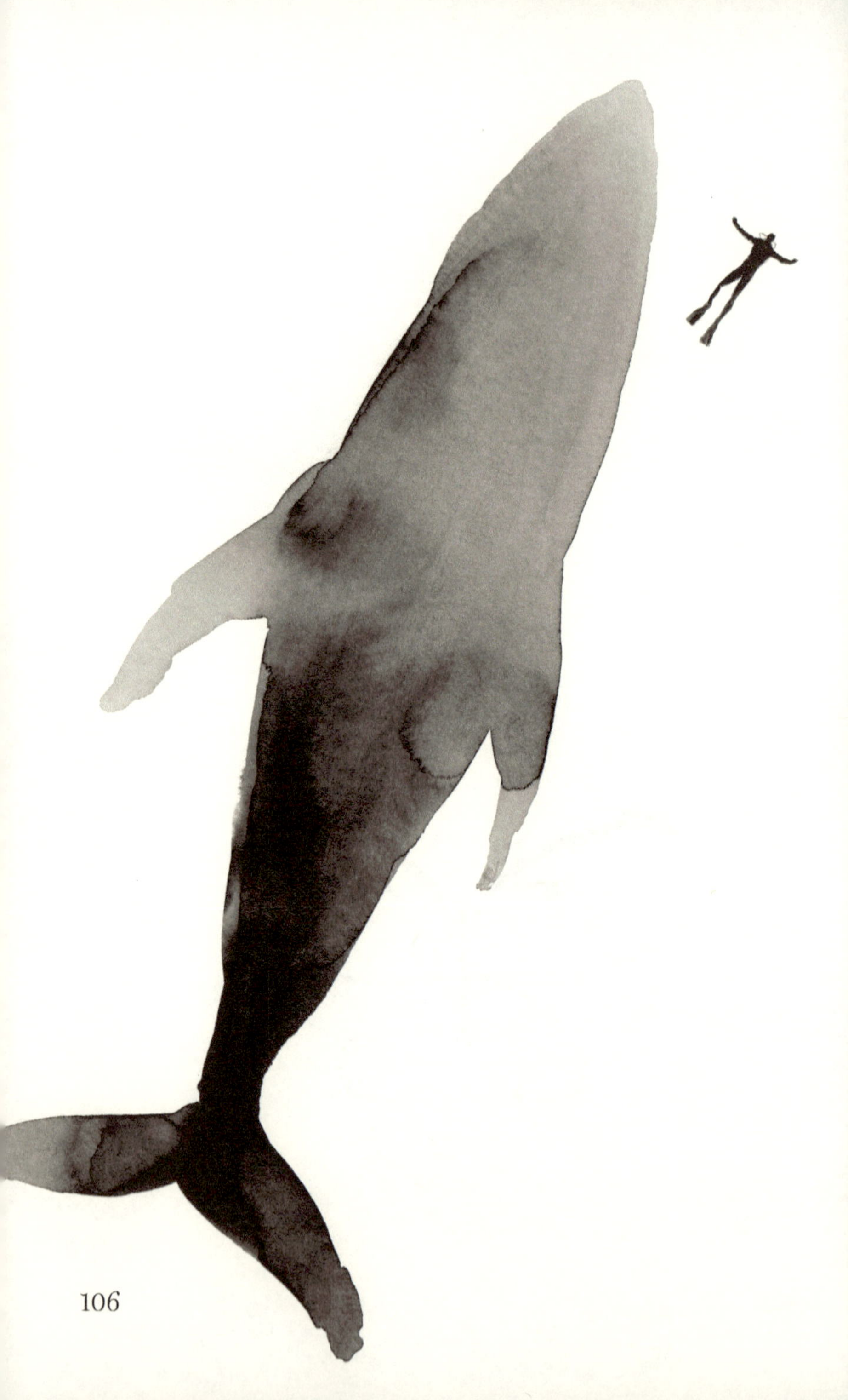

CONCLUSION

Why not depart from life as a sated guest from a feast?
Lucretius, *De rerum natura*[14]

During the disease, I lived at the mercy of my compulsions. I was just a pawn in my own mind's destructive game. All my senses were numb: I was blind to the real image of my own body, and I was deaf to the warnings of all those who tried to help me.

My body was just a marionette in some wicked puppeteer's ghoulish play, and that puppeteer was no other than my anorexic mind, which almost succeeded in achieving its deadly goal.

At that time, I couldn't see what was really going on, I wasn't aware that we are always controlled by our mind — that the thoughts, fears, ideas, beliefs, obsessions and passions that we hold in our mind shape our whole life, day in, day out.

It took years of pain and a near-death experience to lift that veil from my eyes, only to rediscover something that I'd known naturally all the time when I was a child: that life is bliss, and that all the obstacles that prevent us from realizing our happiness stem from our own mind.

Sad even to say it, but just like the children born inside a prison who have never been free are not aware of the wonderful world outside, I too had become so used to living confined in the somber dungeon of anorexic behaviors that I had forgotten that there is a life outside of it. The vision of my own corpse brought about the awareness that shattered the walls of my mental jail, opening the way to a happy life in the eternity of the present. And there is no freedom without awareness, for before you can break out of any prison, you must first realize that you are locked up inside. In the presence of Death, the dark ghosts of my obsessions and repressions vanished in the haze, just like the uncanny characters in a nightmare fade away in the morning light.

Death is the great equalizer. In front of her everything loses its value — everything but life.

The rich and the poor, the healthy and the sick, the strong and the weak… all become one and the same.

Learn to live with death: all your tribulations, no matter how deep, will also vanish in her presence, and all you'll be left with is your bare being. That's when you'll be weighed in the balance of your own conscience, and find out whether you have squandered your best gift, your life, worrying about petty issues, or worse, about an imaginary future which ends without ever having existed. And that's when your conscience will also question you about the talents you were gifted with when you were born; the talents that never brought light to the world because you buried them out of fear; the talents that will now sink with you in the eternal darkness of death.

As far as each one of us is concerned, the whole universe is an expression of our own minds, for nothing can exist for us unless we experience it. And since we only experience in the present, everything — the past, the future, our whole life — can only exist in the present. And death is the end of that present. Then there is no more.

Finally, the big question that has always haunted humanity — whether there's life after death — is inconsequential for our goal, which is the enjoyment of happiness here and now. If there is a life after death, great, so be it, and we will all eventually get there anyway, but since there is nothing we can do about it now, just let it be, and don't rush to get there before your time has come.

What really matters is whether there is a life *before* death. Don't sacrifice your present happiness on the altar of a future bliss that is no more than a prospect, and concentrate instead on the real life you are living now, on your present happiness. The decision is in your hands, for only you can choose to live fully every single moment of your life. The rest is just an illusion.

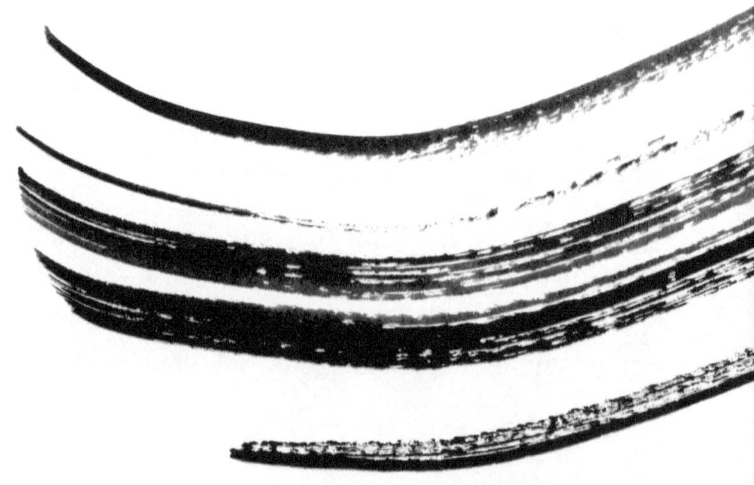

Epilogue

My dear children,

we have now reached the end of our journey together. It's time to bid farewell, but before we part, never forget that there's a mighty wonderful world out there for the taking! And it's waiting for you. So close this book, go out there, and get a life!

Do it now, before it's too late.

Enjoy!

Gijón, Spain, September 9th, 2018

References

[1] **HARDY, THOMAS.** *Jude the obscure.* Harper & Brothers, New York, 1896.

[2] **MONTAIGNE, MICHEL EYQUEM DE.** *Essays of Michel de Montaigne.* Translated by Charles Cotton. Edited by William Carew Hazlitt, A. L. Burt, New York, 1877.

[3] *The teaching of Buddha.* ©1966 by Bukkyo Dendo Kyokai, Tokyo, 1991.

[4] **BARUCH, BERNARD MANNES.** as quoted by Bennett Cerf in *Shake Well Before Using: A New Collection of Impressions and Anecdotes Mostly Humorous.* Garden City Publishing Co., New York, 1950.

[5] **TWAIN, MARK.** *Three thousand years among the microbes.* 1905.

[6] **MACHIAVELLI, NICCOLÒ.** *The Prince.* Translated by W. K. Marriott. Edited by Ernest Rhys. Published in Everyman's Library by J.M. Dent & Sons Ltd., London, and by E.P. Dutton & Co., New York, 1908.

[7] CASANOVA, GIACOMO GIROLAMO. *Mémoires de J. Casanova de Seingalt, écrits par lui-même.* Garnier Frères, Paris, 1880. Translated by Alberto Vezendi from the original French.

[8] THE ROYAL COLLEGE OF PSYCHIATRISTS. *Management of Really Sick Patients with Anorexia Nervosa (MARSIPAN). A Report by Royal Colleges of Psychiatrists, Physicians and Pathologists of the United Kingdom.* © 2014 The Royal College of Psychiatrists, United Kingdom. https://www.rcpsych.ac.uk/pdf/CR189_a.pdf. Used by permission. All rights reserved worldwide.

[9] *The Holy Bible.* New International Version®, NIV® ©1973, 1978, 1984, 2011 by Biblica Inc.® Used by permission. All rights reserved worldwide.

[10] MILTON, JOHN. *Paradise lost.* (1667). Samuel Simmons, London, 1667.

[11] AURELIUS, MARCUS. *Meditations. From The Thoughts of the Emperor Marcus Aurelius Antoninus.* Translated by George Long in 1862. Little, Brown, and Company, Boston, 1889.

[12] TAGORE, RABINDRANATH. *The gardener.* Translated by the author from the original Bengali. The Macmillan Company, New York, 1913.

¹³ **Thoreau, Henry David.** *Walden; or, Life in the Woods.* Ticknor & Fields, Boston, 1854.

¹⁴ **Titus Lucretius Carus.** *De rerum natura* (III, 951). As quoted by Montaigne in *Essays of Michel de Montaigne.* Translated by Charles Cotton. Edited by William Carew Hazlitt, A. L. Burt, New York, 1877.

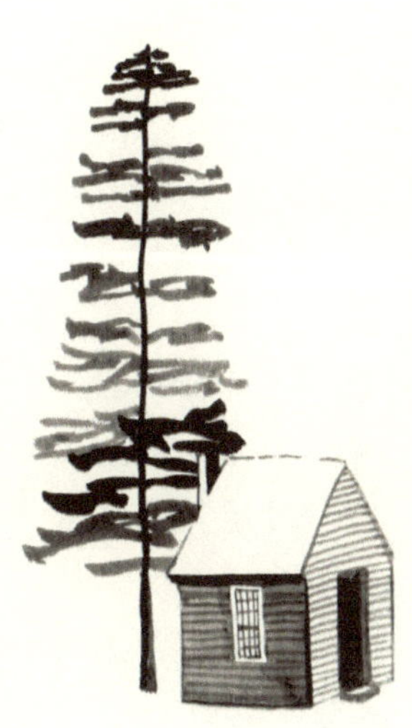

About the Author

A rolling stone gathers no moss. In 1979, at the age of six, Alberto Vezendi was uprooted from the Great Hungarian Plain and planted in Spain, amidst the wonderful beaches and sharp peaks of Asturias. However, instead of roots he grew wings, spread them wide and spent his summers travelling around Europe, mostly on his own, until he finally soared away from the nest. He left Spain in 1998 after finishing his university studies and settled in Paris. There he started a career as a conference interpreter that would take him to more than thirty countries around the world. For the next fifteen years his life was divided between Paris, Brussels, Gijón and Budapest, until in 2013 he landed on the serene shores of Lake Geneva, where he still lives today.

In 2018, after twenty years of being somebody else's voice, he decided to be his own and embarked on a new journey as a writer. This book is one step on that journey.

Vezendi BOOKS